RENOVATE

LEADER GUIDE

Renovate
Building a Life with God

Renovate
978-1-5018-4336-5
978-1-5018-4337-2 *eBook*

Renovate: Leader Guide
978-1-5018-4338-9
978-1-5018-4339-6 *eBook*

Renovate: DVD
978-1-5018-4340-2

The Connected Life
Small Groups That Create Community

This handy and helpful guide describes how churches can set up, maintain, and nurture small groups to create a congregation that is welcoming and outward-looking. Written by Jacob Armstrong with Rachel Armstrong, the guide is based on the pioneering small group ministry of Providence United Methodist Church in Mt. Juliet, Tennessee.

978-1-5018-4345-7
978-1-5018-4346-4 *eBook*

Also by Jacob Armstrong:

Interruptions
Loving Large
The God Story
Treasure: A Four-Week Study on Faith and Money
Upside Down

With Jorge Acevedo:
Sent: Delivering the Gift of Hope at Christmas

With James W. Moore:
Christmas Gifts That Won't Break: Expanded Edition with Devotions

With Adam Hamilton and Mike Slaughter:
The New Adapters

RENOVATE
BUILDING A LIFE WITH GOD

Leader Guide by
Martha Bettis Gee

JACOB ARMSTRONG

Abingdon Press
Nashville

Renovate
Leader Guide

Scripture quotations, unless noted otherwise, are taken from the Holy Bible, New International Version®, NIV®. Copyright © 1973, 1978, 1984, 2011 by Biblica, Inc.™ Used by permission of Zondervan. All rights reserved worldwide. www.zondervan.com The "NIV" and "New International Version" are trademarks registered in the United States Patent and Trademark Office by Biblica, Inc.™

17 18 19 20 21 22 23 24 25 26— 10 9 8 7 6 5 4 3 2 1

MANUFACTURED IN THE UNITED STATES OF AMERICA

CONTENTS

TO THE LEADER

Welcome! In this study, you have the opportunity to help a group of learners explore how they could open their lives to the possibility of being rebuilt by God. In the process of being renovated by God's gracious action, learners may discover how their lives can be more fully lived for God. The study is based on Jacob Armstrong's book, *Renovate: Building a Life with God*.

Armstrong, founding pastor of Providence Church, a United Methodist congregation in Mt. Juliet, Tennessee, tells us that his own renovation began with a question, a breakdown, and a commitment. The commitment introduced him to Nehemiah, and it set Armstrong on a journey he is still on today. Nehemiah's story of renovation, says Armstrong, is his story. It is his belief that God also has a renovation in store for all of us.

Scripture tells us that where two or three are gathered together, we can be assured of the presence of the Holy Spirit, working in and through all those gathered. As you prepare to lead, pray for that presence and expect that you will experience it.

Renovate is one of several small group studies in Jacob Armstrong's series "The Connected Life." The Renovate study includes six sessions and makes use of the following components:

- the book *Renovate: Building a Life with God* by Jacob Armstrong;
- a DVD with a video for each book chapter;
- this Leader Guide.

Participants in the study will also need Bibles, as well as either a spiral bound notebook for a journal or an electronic means of journaling, such as a tablet. If possible, notify those interested in the study in advance of the first session. Make arrangements for them to get copies of the book so that they can read the introduction and chapter 1 before the first group meeting.

Groups may also want to read an optional book, *The Connected Life: Small Groups That Create Community*, by Jacob Armstrong with Rachel Armstrong. The people of Providence Church believe passionately that small groups, even more than worship, form the foundation of their community.

In this little book, churches can learn what makes the Providence small groups unique and can receive guidance for setting up a vibrant small group ministry of their own.

Using This Guide with Your Group

Because no two groups are alike, this guide has been designed to give you flexibility and choice in tailoring the sessions for your group. The session format is listed below. You may choose any or all of the activities, adapting them as you wish to meet the schedule and needs of your particular group.

The leader guide offers a basic session plan for each week designed to be completed in about forty-five minutes.

Select ahead of time which activities the group will do, for how long, and in what order. Depending on which activities you select, there may be special preparation needed. The leader is alerted in the session plan when advance preparation is needed. Here is the session format:

Planning the Session

Session Goals
Scriptural Foundation
Special Preparation

Getting Started

Opening Activity
Opening Prayer

Learning Together

Video Study and Discussion
Book and Bible Study and Discussion

Wrapping Up

Closing Activity
Closing Prayer

Helpful Hints

Preparing for the Session

- Pray for the leading of the Holy Spirit as you prepare for the study. Pray for discernment for yourself and for each member of the study group.
- Before each session, familiarize yourself with the content. Read the *Renovate* chapter again.
- Choose the session elements you will use during the group session, including the specific discussion questions you plan to cover. Be prepared, however, to adjust the session as group members interact and as questions arise. Prepare carefully, but allow space for the Holy Spirit to move in and through the group members and through you as facilitator.
- Prepare the room where the group will meet so that the space will enhance the learning process. Ideally, group members should be seated around a table or in a circle so that all can

see each other. Movable chairs are best because the group will often be forming pairs or small groups for discussion.

- Bring a supply of Bibles for those who forget to bring their own. Also bring writing paper and pens for those participants who do not bring a journal or a tablet or other electronic means of journaling.
- For most sessions you will also need a chalkboard and chalk, a whiteboard and markers, or an easel with large sheets of paper and markers.

Shaping the Learning Environment

- Begin and end on time.
- Create a climate of openness, encouraging group members to participate as they feel comfortable.
- Remember that some people will jump right in with answers and comments, while others need time to process what is being discussed.
- If you notice that some group members seem never to be able to enter the conversation, ask them if they have thoughts to share. Give everyone a chance to talk, but keep the conversation moving. Moderate to prevent a few individuals from doing all the talking.
- Communicate the importance of group discussions and group exercises.
- If no one answers at first during discussions, do not be afraid of silence. Count silently to ten, then say something such as, "Would anyone like to go first?" If no one responds, venture an answer yourself and ask for comments.
- Model openness as you share with the group. Group members will follow your example. If you limit your sharing to a surface level, others will follow suit.
- Encourage multiple answers or responses before moving on.

- To help continue a discussion and give it greater depth, ask, "Why?" or "Why do you believe that?" or "Can you say more about that?"
- Affirm others' responses with comments such as "Great" or "Thanks" or "Good insight," especially if it's the first time someone has spoken during the group session.
- Monitor your own contributions. If you are doing most of the talking, back off so that you do not train the group to listen rather than speak up.
- Remember that you do not have all the answers. Your job is to keep the discussion going and encourage participation.

Managing the Session

- Honor the time schedule. If a session is running longer than expected, get consensus from the group before continuing beyond the agreed-upon ending time.
- Involve group members in various aspects of the group session, such as saying prayers or reading the Scripture. Note that the session guides sometimes call for breaking into smaller groups or pairs. This gives everyone a chance to speak and participate fully. Mix up the groups; don't let the same people pair up for every activity.
- As always in discussions that may involve personal sharing, confidentiality is essential. Group members should never pass along stories that have been shared in the group. Remind the group members at each session: Confidentiality is crucial to the success of this study.

1

NEVER TOO LATE FOR A RENOVATION

Planning the Session

Session Goals

As a result of conversations and activities connected with this session, group members should begin to:

- explore Scriptures that present the metaphor of persons as spiritual houses, in need of God's restoring and renovating work;
- examine barriers to opening themselves to God's renovation;
- encounter key hallmarks of renovation;
- reflect on where they are in need of God's renovation.

Scriptural Foundation

You also, like living stones, are being built into a spiritual house.

(1 Peter 2:5)

Special Preparation

- Have available a notebook or paper along with pen or pencil for anyone who did not bring a notebook or an electronic device for journaling.
- On a large sheet of paper or a board, print the following for the opening activity: Describe what happened in the renovation or remodeling of the house. Did everything go exactly as planned? If not, what were the challenges? frustrations? surprises?
- Also print the following on paper or a board: Will you go wherever I want you to go?
- For the activity on identifying what a renovation looks like, jot down the following on a sheet of paper or a board: foundation, looks strong, is beautiful, is different, requires care.
- For the closing activity, obtain copies of either "Take My Life and Let It Be" or "The Summons" to read or sing together. Music for both hymns can be found online.

Getting Started

Opening Activity

As participants arrive, welcome them to the study.

Gather together. If participants are not familiar with one another, provide name tags and make introductions.

With a show of hands, ask participants to indicate if they have ever been involved in a project to renovate or remodel a house, condominium, or apartment. If the group includes several persons who have been a part of a renovation or remodeling project, ask each of these participants to pair up or form small groups with others who have never been a part of a renovation. Ask them to discuss the posted questions together. (If the group is small and there is only one experienced renovator, discuss the questions in the large group.)

After allowing a few minutes for discussion, ask one or two volunteers to briefly report one incident or aspect of what happened in the course of the project. Encourage the group to make observations about the process of renovation. Then ask:

- What if the project in need of renovation is ourselves?
- What do you think might be the challenges and pitfalls in a spiritual renovation?
- What might be required in order to be spiritually renovated?

Tell the group members that through encountering the experiences of Nehemiah in this study, they will have the opportunity to open themselves to the work of spiritual renovation that only God can do.

Opening Prayer

Pray together, using the following prayer or one of your own choosing:

We come together, O Holy One, to encounter you in a story of renovation. As spiritual houses, we know we are in need of rebuilding our broken places so we can respond to your call. Guide us as we seek to open ourselves more fully to you. In the name of Jesus we pray. Amen.

Learning Together

Video Study and Discussion

In this study, Jacob Armstrong uses the lens of the Book of Nehemiah to explore the idea of spiritual renovation. In session 1, Armstrong uses passages from the Epistles to introduce us to the metaphor of ourselves as spiritual houses. He suggests that, like fixer-upper houses, we are in need of renovation—not as do-it-yourself projects, but through the graceful action only God can work in our lives.

- Armstrong relates the story of how as a college sophomore he was part of a team that worked on house repair and renovation for low-income persons. What did the team discover about Barbara's house, and how did you respond?

- He tells us that it would have been a waste of time to repair the roof if the team had not considered the inside of Barbara's house, which required the skills of professionals to address. How much time and energy do you expend in keeping up the face you present to the world? In what ways, if at all, are you dealing with your spiritual interior?
- We hear that hoarding behavior often has its origin in a traumatic event. Do you believe this is true? In your own life, can you name an event or set of experiences that have caused you to hoard destructive attitudes or behaviors? What aspects of yourself as a fixer-upper do you have difficulty letting go of?

Book and Bible Study and Discussion

Explore a Question

Call the group's attention to the posted question: Will you go wherever I want you to go? If participants have not yet had the opportunity, allow a few minutes for them to quickly scan the introduction and chapter 1. Discuss:

- When author Jacob Armstrong tells us about his experience with this question, it wasn't really about a physical place or a new job or a great life accomplishment on the horizon. What was it about?
- After relating his own story of being confronted by the question and experiencing a kind of breakdown, the author tells about encountering insights through the story of Nehemiah. He observes that Nehemiah's renovation wasn't just about him. Rather, stories of spiritual renovation such as Nehemiah's are always about the renovation of God's people. How do you respond? Do you agree?
- How was the author affected by Andrew, the young man whose story he relates at the beginning of chapter 1? What, in your opinion, does his experience with Andrew show us about the value of sharing spiritual renovation with others?

Explore a Scriptural Metaphor

To prepare for hearing God's word in Scripture, note for participants that the author of First Peter is speaking to the whole church. The same is true of Paul's letter to the Corinthians. The Corinthian church had been experiencing growing pains, and Paul applies the metaphor of a building to the whole church community. Jacob Armstrong extends the metaphor, suggesting that we apply it to ourselves as individuals.

With this in mind, ask the group to listen as a volunteer reads aloud the scriptural foundation passage, 1 Peter 2:5, as well as 1 Corinthians 3:9-10, 16.

Point out that if we embrace the image of spiritual houses to describe ourselves, as Armstrong invites us to do, then we can begin to consider what renovation work we each might need.

Examine Key Barriers to Spiritual Renovation

Explain that in order to be ready for a spiritual renovation, we must first look at barriers we may encounter. First, we need to know where to start.

Ask a volunteer to briefly summarize what the author has to say about his own home and entertaining unexpected guests. Then invite participants to think about the state of their own home, apartment, or living space at this moment. Ask them to visualize the condition as they left it to come to this study. Ask them to jot down in their journals, as best they can recall, what a visitor would see in each room if that person were able to open the door and walk in right now. Then ask participants to jot down what changes they would make, if any, given thirty minutes' warning before the visitor rang the doorbell.

Ask one or two volunteers to report on the state of their home, apartment, or living space and what they would need or want to do to receive visitors. Discuss:

- What do you think your place in its present state would communicate to others?

- To what room or area within it would you close the door before company arrived, regardless of whether you had time to tidy up the main areas?

Ask participants to apply the metaphor of a house to their own interior lives. In silence, invite them to consider:

- What aspects of my spiritual "interior" would I be reluctant to disclose to others? Why?
- What aspects would be easier to share? Why?

Encounter Key Hallmarks

The author uses the example of Chip and Joanna Gaines and their hit television show *Fixer Upper*, as well as the current fascination with do-it-yourself projects, to flesh out an understanding of what a spiritual renovation project might involve. Ask one or two volunteers to briefly summarize the author's story of working on Barbara's home when he was doing renovation and repair work on homes in lower-income neighborhoods. Discuss:

- Why was Barbara unable to do the necessary work herself of cleaning out her house?
- What does this story have to say about what is *not* a part of spiritual renovation work? Who is doing the renovation—for Barbara and for us?

Explain that in order to understand spiritual renovation, we need to know what the hallmarks of such a renovation are. Call attention to the posted sheet with some hallmarks listed: foundation, looks strong, is beautiful, is different, requires care. Form pairs or small groups, and assign one of the listed hallmarks to each (in a very small group, assign to individuals). Ask pairs or small groups to read over what the book has to say about their assigned hallmark.

Back in the large group, ask pairs or small groups to report on their discussion. Then invite them to make observations about how the hallmarks might be interrelated. Discuss, for example, some of the following:

- In your opinion, is it possible for a renovation to be beautiful if it is not strong? Why or why not?
- How would you define *beautiful* in the context of spiritual renovation?
- Can a renovation be strong or beautiful if one does not take care doing it?
- Do you think a renovation must always be different from the original structure? Why or why not?

Reflect on the Need for Renovation.

Remind the group of the earlier activity in which they silently considered the state of the rooms or spaces where they live. Ask them to recall how they evaluated their house. For some participants, perhaps the main rooms are company-ready at this moment, but the bedrooms and bathrooms are a mess. For others, the whole house might look, at the very least, lived in. For a few, perhaps the whole house is orderly, but spaces like the garage or basement are messy or drawers and closets are in disorder.

Invite them now to revisit the questions they considered in silence:

- What aspects of my spiritual "interior" would I be reluctant to disclose to others? Why?
- What aspects would be easier to share? Why?

Wrapping Up

Recall for the group that it is never too late for a renovation. Armstrong illustrates this truth with his story of Jamie, his middle school friend, who was able to turn his life around with God's help and embrace sobriety. Invite participants to consider the interiors of their own spiritual houses as they ponder Armstrong's suggestions for reflection from the close of the chapter:

- Maybe things are really messy inside.
- Maybe it would be embarrassing to expose the mess. Certainly easier to keep the door closed.
- Maybe you don't know where to start.
- Maybe you're like I was and have become so religious that you've forgotten how exciting it is to watch Jesus do what he came to do.

Encourage the group to reflect on these statements and to continue reflecting on them during the coming days.

Remind the group to read chapter 2 before the next session.

Closing Activity

Sing a Hymn

Hand out copies of the hymn you chose before the session, either "Take My Life and Let It Be" or "The Summons." Invite participants to read or sing the hymn together.

Closing Prayer

Holy God, you have promised to be with us always. As we seek to open ourselves to your renovating, redeeming grace, we trust in that promise. Give us strength of purpose. Guide us on this journey as together we seek to submit our lives to you. For it is in the name of Jesus Christ, our foundation, that we pray. Amen.

2

CRYING AND BUILDING

Planning the Session

Session Goals

As a result of conversations and activities connected with this session, group members should begin to:

- explore the scriptural story of Nehemiah for clues that reveal how renovation takes place;
- examine more key aspects of renovation;
- encounter questions for personal renovation;
- reflect further on where they are in need of God's renovation.

Scriptural Foundation

> *When I heard these things, I sat down and wept. For some days I mourned and fasted and prayed before the God of heaven.*
>
> *(Nehemiah 1:4)*

Special Preparation

- Continue to provide journaling materials for those who did not bring any.
- Even participants who have been regular church attenders all their lives may be a bit hazy about Old Testament history and where Nehemiah's life falls in the scope of God's story. Either make copies of the Appendix or print the dates on a large sheet of paper and post it.
- In advance of the session, if possible recruit two volunteers for the Scripture reading. Ask one to read Nehemiah 1:1-4 and the other to read verses 5-11 (omitting the final sentence about Nehemiah's role as cupbearer to the king).
- On four large sheets of paper posted at intervals around your space (or in separate locations on a board), write the following questions. Also obtain large self-stick notes or note cards and tape, as well as pens.
  - o What puts tears in the corners of your eyes?
  - o What do you need to say no to?
  - o What do you need to be honest about?
  - o What promise do you need to remind God about so you can remind yourself?

Getting Started

Opening Activity

As participants arrive, welcome them.

Gather together. Ask a volunteer to briefly retell the opening story in chapter 2 about the author's experience when he was dropping his daughters off for the first day of the school year. Invite participants to form pairs and to discuss with their partner a similar time when they were moved to tears.

In the large group, ask participants to name the experience that evoked tears. Remind them that in the introduction to the study, the author reveals that his own personal renovation was initiated when he broke down in tears. Then tell the group that the story of renovation and rebuilding around which this study is organized opens with news that brings Nehemiah to tears.

Opening Prayer

Pray together, using the following prayer or one of your own choosing:

Draw us into a time of attentiveness, O Holy One of Israel. Open our hearts, minds, and spirits to what the story of Nehemiah reveals. Speak to us through Scripture and through our interactions together as we explore your Word more deeply. In the name of Jesus Christ we pray. Amen.

Learning Together

Video Study and Discussion

In session 2, we begin to explore the story of Nehemiah as a lens through which to dig into the idea of God's renovation. We learn that even though Nehemiah was living in exile, he held a respected and valued position as the king's cupbearer. But in one moment, with one question, Nehemiah was jolted out of his complacent life and brought to tears by the news about Jerusalem.

- Jacob Armstrong relates the story of what happened when he discovered his newly purchased and newly renovated log cabin was in need of further renovation—an expensive surprise no one anticipated. He suggests that something important can happen when everything is in a mess. Do you agree or disagree? Why?
- Can you name a time in your own life when, in a moment, everything changed? Did you experience a season of tears? What happens when you can no longer hide the ramifications of a dire situation? What is the role of honesty in such a situation?
- He notes that when you have tears, you are primed for renovation. How do you respond?

Book and Bible Study and Discussion

Explore the Context

Tell the group that in order to more fully understand Nehemiah's story, it is helpful to understand where this story fits in the history of God's people. Call the group's attention to the Old Testament dates that you posted or that you gave them, and quickly review the span of events that led up to this story. Then ask volunteers to review the information given in the chapter to set the context. Discuss:

- Armstrong observes that Nehemiah's story is set in a time that is reminiscent of our current context. Why?
- Based on what we learn in *Renovate*, what does it mean when Armstrong names Nehemiah as one of the "chosen ones"? Who do you think are the "chosen ones" in our time?
- Nehemiah's people were in exile. Some would say that our people today are experiencing a metaphorical exile. Would you agree? Why or why not? If so, how do you characterize exile? From what are some exiled?

Explore the Story of Nehemiah's Tears

Invite the group to listen as the two volunteers you recruited read Nehemiah 1 aloud. (Recall that one will read verses 1-4, and the other will read verses 5-11, omitting the final sentence about Nehemiah's role as cupbearer to the king.) Give participants a moment or two to review what the author tells us about Nehemiah and about the state of things in Jerusalem. Discuss some of the following together:

- The name *Nehemiah* means "comforted by the Lord." What indications are there that Nehemiah embodied his name? In relation to those who had returned to Jerusalem, how was Nehemiah living?
- We are reminded that Jerusalem had traditionally symbolized the strength of the people and the strength of their God. What

was the significance to the people, literally and metaphorically, that the wall surrounding the city was in disarray?

- If you had to choose a tangible symbol today for God's protection, strength, and care, what would it be? How would you describe its present state and the state of our culture?

Examine More Key Aspects of Renovation

Although Nehemiah was comfortable and seemingly had it made, he was jolted out of his complacent life and brought to tears by the news about Jerusalem. In fact, he cried, prayed, and fasted "for some days." Discuss some of the following:

- The author states that renovation almost always begins with tears. How do you respond to that? When have you been jolted out of complacency by unexpected or uncomfortable news or an unwelcome insight? What did you do?
- What does the author mean when he says that, to move forward, we must say no to the present reality? How did Tanna Clark say no? How did Jamie, the young man with whom Armstrong went to middle school?
- We read that after saying no to the present reality, we can say yes to renovation. Nehemiah was able to envision the future in the midst of brokenness. How do you think it is possible to believe in that future, while at the same time being brutally honest about the reality of that brokenness?
- For Jacob and Rachel Armstrong, what was the concrete symbol of the can't-hide-it-anymore kind of brokenness they experienced when their home required extensive renovation? If you are honest with yourself about the extent of renovation your interior requires, what symbol can you personally identify for that honesty?

Ask someone to reread Nehemiah 1:8-9 aloud. Ask:

- Who needed to be reminded of God's promises?

Encourage participants to consider offering their own prayer similar to Nehemiah's as a way of reminding themselves of God's promises.

Encounter Questions for Personal Renovation

Call the group's attention to the four questions you posted before the session:

- What puts tears in the corners of your eyes?
- What do you need to say no to?
- What do you need to be honest about?
- What promise do you need to remind God about so you can remind yourself?

Jacob Armstrong suggests it might be worth making some space in one's life to ponder these questions. Distribute at least four large self-stick notes or note cards to each participant. Ask them to consider each question and print one or more responses on separate notes/cards. When participants are finished, invite them to attach their responses to the sheet or board beneath each question. Invite them to move around the room reading the responses of others. If they find responses from others that resonate with them, ask them to place a check mark next to that response.

Encourage group members to jot down their own responses and those of others in their journals for further consideration.

Reflect Further on the Need for Renovation

Remind the group of the activities in the previous session in which they compared themselves to a spiritual house. As a way of both reviewing and bringing up to speed any participants not present for the first session, ask one or two volunteers to describe some of the conversation about examining the interiors of our spiritual houses. Direct the group to look back in their journals to the responses they made in the last session to the following questions:

- What aspects of my spiritual "interior" would I be reluctant to disclose to others? Why?
- What aspects would be easier to share? Why?

Invite them now to reflect on what a "sketch" of their renovation might look like. What might God be calling them to say no to? What might they be called to say yes to? Ask participants to record thoughts on these two questions in their journals.

Wrapping Up

Jacob Armstrong tells us that for him personally the most significant of God's promises is that he doesn't have to be afraid. Over and over again in Scripture we read, "Do not be afraid," "Do not fear," and "Be strong and courageous." He suggests that this is God's repeated promise for each of us who needs renovation. Encourage participants to return to these words and to remind God (and themselves) of this comforting promise.

Also encourage participants to read chapter 3 before the next session.

Closing Activity

Armstrong suggests we give serious thought to the questions posed during baptism. While we are most familiar with the final question, the first two questions, called the Renunciation of Sin, also relate directly to God's call to renovation and to our response.

Invite the group to listen as you read aloud the first question asked during baptism, a question that addresses those things to which we are called to say no.

- Do you renounce the spiritual forces of wickedness, reject the evil powers of this world, and repent of your sin?

After allowing a few moments of silence, read aloud the second question, one that addresses those things to which we are called to say yes.

- Do you accept the freedom and power God gives you to resist evil, injustice, and oppression in whatever forms they present themselves?

Encourage the group to attend more closely to these two questions the next time they experience a baptism worship service.

Closing Prayer

Close by offering a prayer similar to the one Armstrong suggests we pray to remind God of God's promises:

God, we know that you said you would never leave us. You said that no matter what we go through, you wouldn't tempt us beyond what we can bear. You said that we are of great value to you, that even if we were in the biggest mess, you would come after us. You said your grace was sufficient for all our messes, that in our weakness your strength is made perfect. We read that you called Nehemiah to a time of crying and praying. Well, that's where we are. But you led Nehemiah back, and he did restore the city. The wall was rebuilt. The people worshiped again. The poor were taken care of and fed. Remember that, God? Yes, we know you remember. Keep our own memories fresh with your enduring promises. In the name of Jesus Christ we pray. Amen

3

WHAT TO KNOW BEFORE YOU BUILD

Planning the Session

Session Goals

As a result of conversations and activities connected with this session, group members should begin to:

- explore the scriptural story of Nehemiah for clues that reveal what they need to know before they can be renovated;
- examine key aspects of renovation they need to know in order to submit themselves to God's renovating power;
- encounter essential questions related to moving forward;
- reflect further on where they are in need of God's renovation.

Scriptural Foundation

I said to them, "You see the trouble we are in:
Jerusalem lies in ruins, and its gates have been burned

with fire. Come, let us rebuild the wall of Jerusalem,
and we will no longer be in disgrace." I also told them
about the gracious hand of my God on me and what
the king had said to me.

They replied, "Let us start rebuilding." So they began
this good work.

(Nehemiah 2:17-18)

Special Preparation

- Continue to provide journaling materials for those who did
  not bring any.
- For the activity on examining further aspects of renovation,
  print the following on a large sheet of paper or a board:
  - o Tell somebody about the dream God has given you for
    renovation.
  - o Renovation is hard.
  - o When God calls you to renovate, God is always preparing
    others, too.
  - o Renovation requires faith.
- If you plan to close by reciting or singing a hymn, locate
  the hymn "How Firm a Foundation" and arrange for
  accompaniment if needed.

Getting Started

Opening Activity

As participants arrive, welcome them.

Gather together. Invite participants to form pairs to discuss the
following:

- Tell about a time when you were a child playing hide-and-seek
  and you were "it." How did you feel when you were searching
  for the other players? What happened?

- Tell about a time when you were playing hide-and-seek and you were hiding. Did you ever hide in a place where no one could find you? What happened?

Sometimes we focus on hide-and-seek as a way of thinking about when we try to run and hide from God, just as Adam and Eve did. But the author wants us to think about the other side of that coin. In this session, we will explore times when it feels as if God is hiding from us and how this relates to renovation.

Opening Prayer

Pray together, using the following prayer or one of your own choosing:

Lead us, O gracious God, as we continue to connect the story of Nehemiah with our own stories. Help us to take the next steps in discerning how we may be rebuilt to be stronger, more loving, and more committed to answering your call. In the name of Jesus we pray. Amen.

Learning Together

Video Study and Discussion

In session 3, we discover the steps Nehemiah began to take once he had fasted, prayed, and agonized over the news that the wall of Jerusalem had been reduced to burned-out rubble, leaving the city and its remaining inhabitants vulnerable and destitute. We read how he engaged in a reconnaissance mission in the dead of night without communicating his intentions to anyone. And we learn how people responded when he finally did tell them.

- The author describes playing hide-and-seek with his daughter. What does he have to say about why God would never hide from us? Has there ever been a time when you felt as though God was hiding from you? What were the circumstances? What happened?

- Armstrong tells us he is glad the narrative includes an account of how Nehemiah explored the city wall at night, torch in hand, without telling anyone. Why? What do we learn from Nehemiah's actions and from how the people responded when he did finally disclose his dream?
- In describing his own journey regarding anxiety, Armstrong describes what happened when he confessed to his parents what he had been experiencing. What does he contend is important about telling other people about your dreams—and your struggles?

Book and Bible Study and Discussion

Explore the Story of Nehemiah's Next Steps

With the help of three volunteers, go through Nehemiah's next steps after fasting, crying, and praying. Invite three volunteers to take the part of Nehemiah and read the three sets of verses below.

Following each reading, ask the group to name, popcorn style, insights that struck them about Nehemiah's motivations and actions.

1. Nehemiah 2:1-10 (He approaches King Artaxerxes and asks permission to go to Jerusalem.)
2. Nehemiah 2:11-16 (He inspects the city walls.)
3. Nehemiah 2:17-18 (He and the others decide to restore the walls.)

Examine Further Aspects of Renovation

Armstrong encourages us to hear from Nehemiah's story that the journey is difficult and God seems quiet at times, but there is a way forward once we hear the call. He suggests there are a few things we need to know in order to submit ourselves to God's renovating power.

Call the group's attention to the four aspects of renovation you posted before the session.

- Tell somebody about the dream God has given you for renovation.
- Renovation is hard.
- When God calls you to renovate, God is always preparing others, too.
- Renovation requires faith.

Form four small groups or pairs and assign one of the aspects to each small group or pair (or in a very small group, assign questions to individual participants). Ask them to refer to both the Scripture passage (Nehemiah 2:1-18) and the information in *Renovate* and be prepared to briefly report on their assigned aspect. After a few minutes' work, come together in the large group and ask each pair or small group to report on their discussion. Ask:

- These aspects or insights about what one needs to know going forward are in many ways counterintuitive in our individualistic, DIY culture. If you had to identify one of these four aspects as the most challenging for you, which one would it be?

Encounter Essential Questions

Call participants' attention to the questions posed in the book to ponder before moving forward:

- Are you struggling to know the next step?
- Are you trying to see what God is up to?
- Where do you need to slow down?
- Whom do you need to tell?

Invite participants to choose one question with which they most resonate at this moment, and spend a few minutes writing a response. If their thoughts generate further questions, ask them to record these for response later, perhaps in a devotional time.

If none of these questions seems on target for a participant, ask the participant to consider another question about renovation that seems the most urgent to her or him, and spend time responding to it.

Reflect on the Need for Renovation

The author posed the following question to two builders: "What's easier—a renovation project or a new build?" Both responded that a new build is easier. A renovation is always more difficult, both builders said, because you have to deal with existing problems rather than starting with a clean slate.

Ask participants to revisit the metaphor of a spiritual house. Ask them to reflect on the following questions, then record thoughts and reactions in their journals.

- Which aspects of my inner life are the most in need of God's renovation?
- Which of these aspects will probably be the most difficult to renovate? Why?
- Are there spiritual walls that must be broken down? stubborn areas resistant to change that must be opened to the fresh breeze of the Spirit? places that need complete gutting and rebuilding?

Wrapping Up

Jacob Armstrong suggests that we tell others about our dream of renovation. Remind the group of God's promise that where two or three are gathered, there God's Spirit will be also. Encourage participants to consider ways in which this group serves as a community of support, discernment, and accountability.

Remind the group to read chapter 4 before the next session.

Closing Activity

Read aloud Hebrews 11:1, which reminds us that restoration is all about faith. After all, in order to renovate, you have to believe in something that you can't yet see. This can be a scary proposition, yet we need not fear. God is faithful, and God's steadfast love is reliable.

Close by singing or reciting together the hymn, "How Firm a Foundation."

Closing Prayer

Amazing God, we trust that the call to renovation is real. Sustain our hope that our lives can be changed. As we seek to move forward, grant us patience and faith. Guide us as we step forward with vulnerability, trusting in your power and grace. In the name of Jesus Christ we pray. Amen.

4

WHEN OTHERS DON'T LIKE YOUR PLANS

Planning the Session

Session Goals

As a result of conversations and activities connected with this session, group members should begin to:

- explore the scriptural story of Nehemiah for clues that reveal how to deal with detractors;
- examine the nature of opposition to rebuilding;
- evaluate the protective value of diligence and memory;
- reflect on where they are encountering resistance as they seek to open themselves to God's renovation.

Scriptural Foundation

> *Tobiah the Ammonite, who was at [Sanballat's] side,*
> *said, "What are they building—even a fox climbing up*
> *on it would break down their wall of stones!"*
>
> *(Nehemiah 4:3)*

Special Preparation

- Provide journaling materials for those who did not bring any.
- On a large sheet of paper or a board, print the following:
  - o   confession and confusion;
  - o   supplication and desperation;
  - o   sustaining presence and listening.
- If you plan to use worship pastor Jenny Youngman's song as a closing, print the lyrics from the chapter on a large sheet of paper or a board.

Getting Started

Opening Activity

Welcome participants as they arrive.

Gather together. Invite the group to reflect in silence on a time when they were told a lie that had serious consequences. Ask them to consider the following:

- Who told the lie? Was it a peer, a teacher, a parent?
- Was the lie communicated verbally or some other way?
- Did you believe the lie? If so, what were the results?

Invite one or two volunteers to tell the group about their experience. Then ask group members to quickly review what the author has to say about the lies the serpent told Adam and Eve, and the resulting consequences of insecurity, loss of vulnerability, and shame.

Tell participants that when we step out to submit to God to make the dream of renovation real, there will be those who tell lies and otherwise place obstacles in our way.

Opening Prayer

Pray together, using the following prayer or one of your own choosing:

Eternal God, we give thanks for the support of those who would stand with us as we seek to make the dream of rebuilding real. Be with us now as we confront the reality of the power of evil. Make us aware of those who would tear us down even as we seek to understand how you can renovate us. Guide our discernment as we open ourselves to your Spirit. In the name of Jesus Christ we pray. Amen.

Learning Together

Video Study and Discussion

In session 4, we learn that in stepping out to submit to God's renovating hand we will encounter those who try to give lie to the truth that our trust is in God. Like Nehemiah and those who were working to rebuild the wall around Jerusalem, as we begin to experience success, the opposition will stiffen and may even become violent. We discover that the protection Nehemiah instituted was the truth of God's desire that we be restored.

- Armstrong relates the rhetoric used by Sanballat and Tobiah as they sought to discredit and discourage Nehemiah and those rebuilding the wall. When, if at all, have you encountered this kind of opposition as you sought to bring a dream to fruition? What kinds of comments did your detractors make? What effect did the comments have on you?
- We read that when the opposition stiffened, Nehemiah kept the trumpeter near at hand so he could rally the workers if the need arose. Armstrong notes that the "trumpet call" used

is not a new one. What examples from Israel's past does he call to our attention? What examples can you give from your history, or from our shared history, when we have had need of the trumpet call?

- Armstrong asserts that the protection Nehemiah used was the truth. How would you describe and express that truth?

Book and Bible Study and Discussion

Explore the Story of Nehemiah's Detractors

Invite someone to reread Nehemiah 2:17-20. Note that in Nehemiah's story, from the start there were detractors and naysayers putting obstacles in the way of rebuilding. Encourage the group to read over Nehemiah 4 and to scan the author's comments in *Renovate*, chapter 4.

After allowing a few moments for participants to review, ask them to form small groups to create a storyline for the passage. In small groups, have them jot down words or phrases as a sort of shorthand for each event in the account. For example, to summarize the initial criticism voiced by Sanballat the Horonite and Tobiah the Ammonite, they might write "fox breaking down a stone wall."

Back in the large group, construct the storyline by having groups list events in turn until all events are listed in order. When all the events are listed, invite participants to make observations or identify insights that came to them from reading the passage or from the author's comments about it, or that arose out of the discussion in their small group. Jot these down beside the storyline.

Examine the Nature of Opposition to Rebuilding

It is inevitable in a renovation project that we will encounter some opposition and that success will breed stiffer opposition as the work begins to bear fruit. Invite participants to look over the storyline. Pose the following questions for consideration. Invite volunteers to respond out loud, then ask others to respond in writing in their journals.

- Where was the initial opposition that Nehemiah encountered? What "tools" did the detractors use at the beginning?
  - o Can you name a time when you began to move forward on a dream God had placed in your heart and others opposed you from the start?
  - o If so, in what form did that opposition come? Was it disparagement, sarcasm, belittlement, or something else?
- When did the opposition stiffen in the rebuilding project God called Nehemiah to do? How did Nehemiah respond?
  - o How have you experienced a stiffening of opposition?
  - o Has it come from someone else, or has it taken the shape of your own personal discouragement or from being tired?

Being Diligent in Prayer, Scripture, and Counsel

We are reminded that early in Nehemiah's story he was diligent in prayer, understanding his people's story in relation to God. Call the group's attention to the list you prepared and posted that identifies the structure of Nehemiah's prayers. Invite participants to write down responses to the following questions in their journals:

- In your own prayer life, where do most of your prayers fall on a continuum from confession to supplication to sustained listening?
- Do you engage in prayer regularly and for a significant period of time?
- What would most help you to deepen your prayer life?

Armstrong also reminds us of the key role that memory plays to ground us in truth. Invite the group to respond to the following in their journals:

- How do you encounter Scripture? Are you involved in regular reading of the Bible? Do you engage systematically with important stories in Scripture, or is your reading more quick and casual?

- What would help you most in broadening and deepening your encounters with Scripture?

Remind participants that Nehemiah began his renovation project by talking with the king, and Nehemiah most likely continued conferring with those who gave wise counsel. Ask participants now to respond to the following in their journals:

- Where and with whom do you seek wise counsel? What groups are you a part of where participants struggle with Scripture and the questions and challenges it surfaces?
- Do you interact with and listen to others of diverse backgrounds and experiences, such as with people of different racial, social, and cultural backgrounds; with political views that differ from yours; or with children, young people, and elderly people?
- What would most help you in extending your access to wise counsel?

Reflect on Discerning the Truth from Lies

To the extent that we can be more diligent in prayer, Scripture, and counsel, we will be better able to recognize lies that can challenge our worth and our hope of experiencing renovation.

Ask participants to form pairs. With their partner, ask them to discuss the third question in each of the three categories (prayer, Scripture, counsel) that they just explored in writing. What would help them most in deepening and extending these three practices?

After allowing a few minutes for partners to discuss, gather together to report questions, insights, and suggestions that grew out of their discussions.

Wrapping Up

Remind the group that Jenny Youngman, a worship pastor at Providence Church where Jacob Armstrong also pastors, wrote a song Armstrong includes in chapter 4, titled "Brave and Strong." Armstrong tells us that this song has become a "trumpet call" for their church as they seek to follow God. Invite participants to complete the following:

- My trumpet call is _____.
- I trust my God will fight for me when_____.

Remind participants to read chapter 5 before the next session.

Closing Activity

Recite the Song Lyrics

Using the lyrics you prepared before the session, ask the group to recite together the lyrics to Jenny Youngman's song "Brave and Strong."

Closing Prayer

Redeeming God, we give thanks that you are a God of rescue! We trust in your transforming power to repair all our broken parts and to crush all the lies of the serpent. We rejoice that you know our whole story—the apples eaten and the insults believed. And now we open our hearts to your continuing renovation, trusting that we might be made more whole. In the name of Jesus Christ we pray. Amen.

5

INVITING OTHERS TO COME HOME

Planning the Session

Session Goals

As a result of conversations and activities connected with this session, group members should begin to:

- explore the scriptural story of Nehemiah for clues that reveal how their own renovation can have an impact on others;
- evaluate the possibilities in their renovations;
- examine the nature of homecoming;
- reflect further on where they are in need of God's renovation.

Scriptural Foundation

My God put it into my heart to assemble the nobles, the officials and the common people for registration by

families. . . . Ezra praised the LORD, the great God; and
all the people lifted their hands and responded, "Amen!
Amen!" Then they bowed down and worshiped the
LORD with their faces to the ground.

(Nehemiah 7:5a; 8:6)

Special Preparation

- Provide journaling materials for those who need them.
- For the activity about homecoming, print the following on three separate large sheets of paper, then post the sheets at intervals around your space, along with felt-tipped markers in two colors.
  - o The people heard that God remembered them. God remembers you.
  - o The people remembered who they were. You must remember who you are.
  - o The people remembered the law. You need to remember God's law.

Getting Started

Opening Activity

Welcome participants as they arrive.

Gather together. Invite someone to describe the Christmas present Jacob Armstrong created for his wife, Rachel. Then ask volunteers to respond to the following questions:

- Have you ever worked so long and so hard on a project that when you completed it, you had a sense of overwhelming joy but also a strange sense of loss? If so, describe the project and what happened.
- How do you account for the conflicting emotions you experienced?

- In what way, if at all, did you have the desire to share what you had done with others?

Nehemiah had devoted much time to planning, working, and building. After the project was finished, he invited the people to share the completed work. Explain that in this session participants will explore how the renovation God is doing in each one of them will likewise soon be shared.

Opening Prayer

Pray together, using the following prayer or one of your own choosing:

Amazing God, we sense the power of your energizing, restless Spirit. As you continue your work of transforming us from within, we find ourselves restless, too—moved to share your power with others. Guide us as we seek ways to do so. In Jesus' name we pray. Amen.

Learning Together

Video Study and Discussion

In session 5, we confront the reality that our own renovation might set in motion an impact on others that we had not imagined possible. After the wall was completed and the doors were set in place, Nehemiah observed that the city, while spacious, was without houses and inhabited by very few people. But the rebuilding of the walls had the effect of making further renovation and rebuilding possible, and Scripture lists all those who came out of exile and returned to rebuild their homes and their lives.

- After relating the story of how he built a coffee table as a present for his wife, Rachel, Jacob Armstrong poses this question for our consideration: Have you ever worked on something for a long time and on completion wondered what to do next? If you've had this experience, did you feel compelled to share the question with others? How did you feel about sharing it?

- He remarks that in renovation, we remember who we are. What does he mean by that statement?
- Armstrong tells of working to help Elaina clear out the rubble of her destroyed home. A woman whose life had been bookended by two great American tragedies, Pearl Harbor and Hurricane Katrina, Elaina nevertheless was confident that she would be able to celebrate the rebuilding of her home. What do you think she could see that Armstrong could not yet see— that is, what memory did she have that Armstrong did not yet have?

Book and Bible Study and Discussion
Explore the Story of Nehemiah's Invitation to the Exiles

To set the context for today's Scripture and to help participants get a sense of how the people had felt in exile, have someone read aloud Psalm 137:1-6. Then invite participants to listen as another volunteer reads aloud Nehemiah 7:1-5a. Discuss some of the following:

- Nehemiah had not rebuilt the whole city; he had simply made further rebuilding seem possible again. If his story is not about a wall being rebuilt, what is it about?
- What does Armstrong suggest is the theme, not just of Nehemiah's story but of the whole Bible?
- Imagine being in Nehemiah's shoes when he walked around the completed wall. What might he have seen? What might he have heard?

Evaluate the Possibilities in Our Renovations

With the walls of Jerusalem rebuilt, Nehemiah had ensured that people could return to live inside those walls in safety and security. In Nehemiah 7, Nehemiah reports the exact number of the returning exiles, including male and female slaves and singers, as well as horses, camels, and donkeys. Then we are invited to imagine what our own renovations might set in motion, and the author suggests that such a possibility is both exciting and risky.

Form two smaller groups. Assign to one group the exploration of what is exciting about the rebuilding of their lives with God, and assign to the other group an exploration of what is risky. Ask each group to discuss the following questions, addressing either what might be exciting or what might be risky:

- Consider the homecoming that is possible through the rebuilding of your life with God. As you begin to experience new life and renewal, who do you think God might invite to come home?
- What is exciting/risky about who could encounter God through your renovated life?

After allowing the two groups to discuss for a few minutes, invite each group to summarize briefly their discussion for the benefit of the other group. Then continue the discussion together in the large group.

- If, as a result of our personal renovations, God expands our horizons beyond what we might have imagined, what changes might result in our life together as a community of faith?
- Are there Sanballats and Tobiahs in our midst? How might they be affected?
- Who are the exiles in our communities—that is, who are the persons who have been gone from the church for a generation, or who have never found a home in a community of faith?

Examine the Nature of Homecoming

Point out that God's renovation project through Nehemiah was an avenue for the people to return, not just to the land from which they had been exiled but all the way back to God's heart.

To set the stage for this next Scripture, explain that Ezra was a scribe and a priest whose concern was to rekindle the memory of the Torah in the people and enforce its observance. Invite a volunteer to read aloud Nehemiah 8:1-6.

Remind the group that in the previous session, they explored the importance of memory—in particular, of remembering the story of God's gracious acts and God's promises that we encounter in Scripture. Call attention to the three sheets of paper you posted around the room and the words on each:

- The people heard that God remembered them. God remembers you.
- The people remembered who they were. You must remember who you are.
- The people remembered the law. You need to remember God's law.

Form three smaller groups or pairs, depending on the size of your group. Assign to each group one of the posted sheets as a starting point. Ask groups to refer to what the chapter says about the biblical text and its meaning for us today. Suggest that they add important points to the sheet with one color of marker, and questions they have with another color.

After allowing time for each group to discuss, ask participants to move around the room, reading the points and questions noted by each of the other two groups. Back in the large group, invite participants to respond to the following:

- As we undergo God's renovation, we should expect to experience the joy of inviting others in. Further, we should look forward to inviting others in, even as we ourselves are in the midst of renovation. Recall the many kinds of people in Nehemiah's story who were invited to return to Jerusalem. With that in mind, name some of the people you'll invite. How will you invite them?
- On our really good days, we hear the Word of God in the same way it was heard by the people coming back to Jerusalem, as if it were the first time. When and where have you experienced that level of anticipation and receptivity on hearing or reading God's Word? In worship? In a study session, such as the ones

you are engaged in now? What sets the stage for experiencing God's word in this way?

- Armstrong tells us the story of Elaina, whose life was bookmarked by the twin tragedies of Pearl Harbor and Hurricane Katrina. He notes that Elaina had learned that when broken things are restored, one of the first things we do is invite others to join us in celebration. What about you? In what ways are you able to trust that God will continue to do the work of rebuilding in you, even when that process is far from completed?

Reflect on God's Renovation

Recall with the group that both Paul and the author of First Peter invited us to consider ourselves to be in some ways like spiritual houses. In chapter 5 of *Renovate*, Christian author C. S. Lewis is quoted as extending that image of God.

Invite a volunteer to read aloud the Lewis quotation. Ask participants to consider various surprises we may encounter—some surprises welcome and some perhaps not so welcome—as God the onsite contractor takes the renovation in directions we may not have anticipated. Ask participants to write in their journals on some of the following:

- Lewis observes that while you may be thinking you will be made into a decent little cottage, God is instead building a palace where he intends to come and live. How do you respond to that concept? Is the idea that your spiritual renovation may be on a grand scale daunting? exciting?
- If we are imagining that our renovation plan has a little chapel off to one side where God can live and be worshiped, we might want to scrap that plan. Why?
- As you consider your own interior life, have you been trying to relegate God to a one-hour-a-week worship service, or to the role of a cosmic rescue service? What are the implications if God desires to dwell in the whole of your house?

- What spiritual "junk" may need to be cleared out so that you will have room for people to come and visit?

Wrapping Up

Renovate, chapter 5, opens with the account of a coffee table that Jacob Armstrong constructed as a Christmas gift for his wife. He felt compelled to share his excitement and pride with others—even if his wife was less than enthusiastic about the table. Later in the chapter Armstrong relates another tale of a table, this one about a beautiful dining room table that was the culmination of a man's dream to build a workshop and that, when used, sparked community and sharing.

Remind participants that the table is a powerful symbol of invitation and reconciliation for us as Christians—a place where all are welcome, no matter where they are in the process of being renovated, and where all can share equally in the gifts of God's grace.

In the coming days, ask participants to consider where they are in God's plan for rebuilding their spiritual houses.

Remind the group to read chapter 6 before the final session.

Closing Activity

Recite a Psalm

In Nehemiah 8, after the renovation was finished, all the people came together in joyful worship to hear the law read and interpreted. Form two groups and have them join in a responsive reading of Psalm 19:7-9, 14:

Group 1:   The law of the LORD is perfect,
        refreshing the soul.

Group 2:   The statutes of the LORD are trustworthy,
        making wise the simple.

Group 1:   The precepts of the LORD are right,
        giving joy to the heart.

Group 2:   The commands of the LORD are radiant,
        giving light to the eyes.

Group 1:   The fear of the LORD is pure,
                 enduring forever.

Group 2:   The decrees of the LORD are firm.
                 and all of them are righteous.

All: **May these words of my mouth and this meditation of my heart be pleasing in your sight,**
                 LORD, my Rock and my Redeemer.

Closing Prayer

O God, our Rock and our Redeemer, through your son you are our foundation and the source of our renovation. Be with us now, as you have promised. Give us further glimpses of the wonderful plan you have for our lives. Amen.

6

THE BIG REVEAL

Planning the Session

Session Goals

As a result of conversations and activities connected with this session, group members should begin to:

- explore the scriptural story of Nehemiah for clues that reveal how to remember the past, celebrate the now, and look to where God is calling them, even in the midst of their renovation;
- encounter aspects of past, present, and future in the celebration of renovation;
- reflect on where they are in the process of being renovated by God;
- celebrate together what has been, what is, and what will be.

Scriptural Foundation

> *On the second day of the month, the heads of all*
> *the families, along with the priests and the Levites,*
> *gathered around Ezra the teacher to give attention to*
> *the words of the Law. They found written in the Law,*
> *which the LORD had commanded through Moses, that*
> *the Israelites were to live in temporary shelters during*
> *the festival of the seventh month.*
>
> *(Nehemiah 8:13-14)*

Special Preparation

- Provide journaling materials for those who need them.
- On a large sheet of paper, print the following:
  - o God turns our hearts to where we have been.
  - o God calls upon us to celebrate the present goodness.
  - o God will turn our hearts to where we are going.
- Choose a hymn to sing or recite at the close of this final session. The hymn "Stand Up and Bless the Lord" is a setting of Nehemiah 9:5. (The text and accompaniment can be found online at www.hymnsite.com.) Or you can choose a familiar hymn of praise instead and arrange for accompaniment, if needed.

Getting Started

Opening Activity

Welcome participants to this final session of the study.

Gather together. Invite participants to form pairs and tell their partner about an episode they remember of *Fixer Upper*, or a similar television show. Try to arrange things so that at least one of the people in each pair has seen the show.

Back in the large group, discuss the following:

- On fixer-upper shows, what is the Big Reveal?
- In the context of faith, what does the Big Reveal call to mind? What does Armstrong's story of Julia tell us about renovation?

Tell participants that in this final session, they will explore more deeply what impact their renovations might have on others.

Opening Prayer

Pray together, using the following prayer or one of your own choosing:

Creating and renewing God, we acknowledge that we are your works in progress. Yet we seek to be a part of your plan, not only for our own ongoing renovations, but for the renewal and restoration of the cosmos. Guide us as we consider what you would have us do. In the name of Jesus Christ. Amen.

Learning Together

Video Study and Discussion

In session 6, we discover that the people responded to rebuilding the wall and their homes in a counterintuitive way: They reclaimed a long-dormant religious festival in which they left their homes and lived in temporary shelters for a time. In doing so, the people were called to remember when they had been exiles, to celebrate the goodness of the present moment, and to look to the future.

- Imagine that your congregation is preparing to celebrate the first worship service in a new sanctuary that the church has long anticipated and needed. Suppose as you come to worship, you find that, instead of entering the new building for the service, a tent has been set up on the lawn for worship. How would you respond? What might such a gesture be communicating about earthly buildings?

- Armstrong tells us that no earthly building is home. What does he mean?
- Why does he suggest that God puts us in what he calls temporary tents—our earthly bodies?

Book and Bible Study and Discussion
Explore the Story of the People's Celebration

Recall for participants that in the previous session, we read in the story of Nehemiah what the people did when the walls were finished and the exiles returned. Invite someone to briefly summarize what they remember from the passage about how Nehemiah and Ezra gathered the people together for worship and to hear the reading of the law.

Ask the group to read aloud Nehemiah 8:13-18 in round-robin style, where people read aloud one verse each and continue around the circle until the passage has been completed.

Invite volunteers to tell what they know about the Festival of Booths. Some may remember building booths in church school when they were children. Ask:

- What does the author tell us about this holiday? What did it commemorate?
- The Jewish people observe a number of holidays and festivals. Why do you think the Feast of the Booths was the one festival chosen for renewal at this particular time in the life of the people?
- What did the people remember? What did they celebrate? What do you imagine they might have been looking forward to in the future?

Encounter Aspects of Past, Present, and Future

Call the group's attention to the three sentences you posted before the session that express three points the author invites us to consider when we, like Nehemiah and the returned exiles, get to the point of celebrating what we have built.

- God turns our hearts to where we have been.
- God calls upon us to celebrate the present goodness.
- God will turn our hearts to where we are going.

Form three small groups. (Alternatively, if your group is very small, do this exercise in the large group.) In each small group, assign the first statement to one person, the second statement to another person, and the third statement to still another person. Ask each person to focus on what the chapter has to say about their assigned statement, then report what they discovered to the others in their group.

Back in the large group, discuss the following:

- What does Armstrong mean when he says it's helpful to remember that, for the people of God, "the meantime" is most of the time?
- For Jacob and Rachel Armstrong, what is the meaning of the phrase *This is our go?*
- What was the somewhat infuriating question that someone asked Jacob on the first Sunday in the new church building, and what did it remind him of?
- In your own experience, which is the most challenging: remembering the past, celebrating the present, or looking to where God is calling you in the future? Why?

Reflect on Progress in the Process of Being Renovated

Ask the group to think back together on the idea that we are spiritual houses being renovated by God's redeeming action. Discuss together:

- Armstrong reminds us that while our spiritual houses are being renovated, we are also living in physical houses—our bodies—that need to be cared for. What has Armstrong learned because of his chronic ailment related to blood clots?
- In what way is the Festival of Booths a reminder of the reality of being human?

Encourage group members to remember or read some of the reflections in their journals from past sessions, keeping in mind that the renovation is ongoing and likely to continue to the end of their lives. Remind them of the C. S. Lewis quotation about surprises we may encounter as God seeks our renovation. Invite them to reflect in writing on the following:

- Where in my spiritual house can I detect that the renovating hand of God has been at work?
- Where in my spiritual house is there still work to be done? What are some things I can do to help God move that work forward?

Wrapping Up

Ask participants to think back over the sessions in this study. Ask them to evaluate the study together by responding, popcorn style, to the following prompts:

- The best thing about this study was…
- Something I would have changed is…
- I found it surprising that…
- One thing that was disturbing or unsettling was…
- In reflecting on my spiritual house, one spiritual practice I intend to continue is…

Invite participants to reflect in silence on the following:

- Right now I would characterize my spiritual house as: still pretty much a shambles; undergoing a major renovation; stripped down to the studs and ready for God's redeeming work; transformed but with work remaining to be done.

Closing Activity

Remind the group that in Nehemiah's story, when the people gathered together they shouted amen, lifted their arms, bowed their heads, and worshiped with their faces to the ground. In Nehemiah 9, following a time of group confession, Ezra recited a long speech giving the history of God's gracious and redemptive acts.

Invite the group to join in the reading of a similar but shorter recitation. Read aloud the first phrase of each verse of Psalm 136, and have participants respond each time by saying, "His love endures forever."

Together, recite or sing "Stand Up and Bless the Lord" or another hymn of your choice.

Closing Prayer

Great and mighty and awesome God, we give thanks that you never give up on us! Grant that we may be receptive to your work of continuing redemption, trusting that we may be rebuilt into spiritual houses worthy of your indwelling. In the name of Jesus Christ, the Word who became flesh and dwelt among us. Amen.

APPENDIX:
OLD TESTAMENT HISTORY

The Unified Monarchy
King Saul (1095 B.C. – 1015 B.C.)
King David (1015 B.C. – 970 B.C.)
King Solomon (970 B.C. – 930 B.C.)
The Kingdom Splits (930 B.C.)

Israel
Israel, the Northern Kingdom (930 B.C. – 725 B.C.)
Assyria destroys Israel (725 B.C.)

Judah
Judah, the Southern Kingdom (930 B.C. – 590 B.C.)
Nineveh, the capital of Assyria, destroyed (612 B.C.)
Babylonian Exile (590 B.C.)

Exile in Babylon
King Nebuchadnezzar of Babylon (605 B.C. – 562 B.C.)
King Cyrus of Persia (576 B.C. – 530 B.C.)
Jews start returning to Jerusalem (536 B.C.)
Temple Rebuilt (530 B.C. – 515 B.C.)

The Connected Life
Small Groups That Create Community

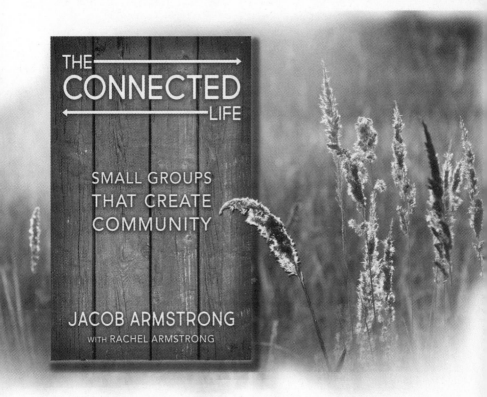

This handy and helpful guide describes how churches can set up, maintain, and nurture small groups to create a congregation that is welcoming and outward-looking.

Written by founding pastor Jacob Armstrong with Rachel Armstrong, the guide is based on the pioneering small group ministry of Providence United Methodist Church in Mt. Juliet, Tennessee.

978-1-5018-4345-7
978-1-5018-4346-4 eBook

 Abingdon Press™

Available wherever fine books are sold.